First Lyons Press Edition: August 2000

Printed in China

10 9 8 7 6 5 4 3 2 1

The Library of Congress Cataloging-in-Publication Data
is available on file.

Contents

5

Introduction

9

The Flavor of Pheasant Hunting

by Steve Grooms

65

The Ringneck in North America:
A Brief History

by Russ Sewell & Dave Nomsen

73

A Year in the Life:
The Ringneck's Natural History

by Russ Sewell

INTRODUCTION

I didn't get much exposure to hunting when I was a boy growing up in Brooklyn, New York. In fact, there was not one sportsman in my family. But that didn't thwart my enthusiasm. I read magazines such as *Field & Stream*, *Outdoor Life* and *Sports Afield*, and became fascinated with the thought of hunting for pheasants. I daydreamed about it for many years.

Finally, when I was sixteen, a friend's father asked us if we wanted to go bird hunting with him. Without hesitation I said, "You bet!" The next Sunday morning, we were on a farm in upstate New York, hunting for ringneck pheasants. I thought I had died and gone to heaven. After all the long years of waiting and dreaming, I was actually afield, holding a loaded shotgun and hunting. I can remember gazing across the autumn landscape and thinking, "It just doesn't get any better than this!"

The image of the first ringneck I shot that day is still etched in my mind. I was walking through thick cover and the cockbird exploded from the underbrush just yards to my left. For a brief moment, its cackling and beauty mesmerized me. I quickly regained my senses as my friend shouted over, "Point and shoot! Point and shoot!" The No. 6 pellets caught the brilliantly colored cockbird as it flew broadside. It went down some 30 yards away. When I picked it up, two lifelong memories were instantly imprinted in my mind. First, I had just shot something that was alive moments ago. From that moment on, I decided not to take that responsibility lightly. The second memory wasn't as profound, but it was equally overpowering. "So this is hunting!" I was hooked! I read every book

and article I could get my hands on about hunting pheasants. I was thoroughly educated by the writings of Gene Hill, Charlie Waterman, Jim Fergus, Phil Bourjaily, John Barsness, and Tom Huggler, to name a few.

For the past thirty-eight years, I've been blessed to hunt just about every game animal in North America. Although I am primarily a whitetail hunter now, I have always held a special place in my heart and mind for the ringneck pheasant. Despite the accolades given to grouse and woodcock by many bird hunters, ringnecks remain a most exciting challenge to me. Each time a cockbird sings its song of excitement as it flushes in front of a dog, or bursts like a rocket from thick tangles that would impair a sparrow, or streaks toward the sky after being routed from a standing cornfield, my heart blissfully misses a beat.

No, the pheasant is not a wily ruffed grouse or woodcock—it's just a transplant—like most of us. But it has captured the hearts, minds and imaginations of many a hunter. The ringneck pheasant has blessed me with the absolute pleasure of pursuing it through muddy fields; cold, wet swamps, and deep narrow ditches, just in hopes of hearing or seeing one break out from cover in front of me. Whether I was successful or not, I came away a better person. For this alone, I will always owe a debt of gratitude to the ringneck pheasant as found in the pages of this book. I hope you, too, can form as strong a bond with such a worthy adversary.

PREFACE

As a boy growing up in the 1960s, the opening day of pheasant season was akin to Christmas morning for me. The first steps afield marked the culmination of months of pent-up anticipation, of gleaning the pages of outdoor magazines, of clay bird shoots, and reloading shotgun shells. The meanings of those hunts are all but inexpressible and only understood by those whose souls have been pervaded by the infatuation of hunting wild ringnecks.

The pheasant is unlike any other gamebird we have in North America. He's crafty, and just when you think you've pinned him down, he's gone. While quail often sit politely beneath the quivering nose of a pointing dog, the desperado rooster pheasant sneaks off, leaving both pointer and handler in a state of disbelief. I've seen flushing dogs ready to tear their tails off keeping up with a bird that can run faster than the notorious roadrunner. With all this frustration, why do we love this less-than-gentlemanly quarry? Because, like baseball, bluegrass music, and apple pie, hunting ringnecks is uniquely American, a challenge that ties us to our past.

Since the pheasant's introduction to America in 1882, it has witnessed the transformation of the landscape by agriculture. Likewise, pheasant hunting has also changed from being the passion of depression-era farm boys to that of suburban-dwelling computer jockeys. Through all this change, though, the pheasant remains a barometer of land health.

Despite almost a century of land use that has caused pheasant populations to peak and to plummet, as well as changes within our society that have distanced us from the land, hunting ringnecks today remains the passion of four million Americans. It is hoped that through this book the reader will gain a greater appreciation for the bird's needs, its history, and its future, which are inseparably tied to the American farmer and pheasant hunter.

—by Russ Sewell
Pheasants Forever

RING-NECKED PHEASANT, WESTERN MONTANA. *Alan & Sandy Carey*

A COCK PHEASANT IS UNDOUBTEDLY THE ORNERIEST, MOST CONTEMPTIBLE, LOW-DOWN, MISERABLE BIRD THAT A HUNTER EVER HAD TO CONTEND WITH. THERE'S NO TRICK HE DOESN'T KNOW OR WON'T USE. WHERE POSSIBLE HE'LL DROP HIS HEAD AND TAIL TO THE GROUND AND SNEAK AWAY LIKE A THIEF IN THE NIGHT, MIRACULOUSLY INCONSPICUOUS EVEN IN THIN COVER; IF HE CAN SEE HIS WAY CLEAR, HE'LL DIG IN AND WITH HEAD AND TAIL HIGH AND RUN LIKE A RACE HORSE; HE'LL SQUAT WITHIN TWO FEET OF A HUNTER'S FEET AND LET THE MAN WALK RIGHT PAST HIM; AND HE'LL FLY ONLY WHEN CORNERED—A RARE THING—OR WHEN IT IS STRICTLY TO HIS ADVANTAGE. AND WHEN HE DOES JUMP, HE'LL DO SO WITH A FLASH OF COLOR AND A RAUCOUS CACKLE THAT WILL THROW A MAN'S TIMING ABOUT TWENTY DEGREES OFF CENTER.

ALL OF WHICH IS HIGH PRAISE.
MORE POWER TO HIM.

Dan Holland, *The Upland Gamehunter's Bible*

by Steve Grooms

THE FLAVOR OF PHEASANT HUNTING

Any form of upland hunting has much in common with any other. There will be a landscape, a bird, and a hunter with a shotgun. If that hunter is serious about his sport, there will also be a dog. That is upland hunting, no matter which bird is the centerpiece of the hunt.

And yet each upland hunt has its unique flavor, a flavor as distinct as scotch is from gin, or indeed as blackberry brandy is from buttermilk. Quail, prairie grouse, woodcock, Hungarian partridge, ruffed grouse, pheasants . . . each is unique and wonderful in its own way.

Yes, but what makes pheasant hunting special, so unlike other forms of upland hunting? The question isn't as easy as it might sound.

⋆⇒ ⇐⋆

HUNTER SURPRISED BY FLUSHING ROOSTER.
Dale C. Spartas

WORKING A THORN APPLE THICKET FOR RINGNECKS. *Dale C. Spartas*

Weather provides part of the answer.

Pheasant hunting weather is more harsh than mellow, more melancholy than pretty, more masculine than feminine. In true pheasant weather, the rest of the family stays indoors while the pheasant hunter stumbles through snowbanks with hands so numb that, should a rooster explode from the cover, his thumbs might not be able to move the safety of his gun.

Of course, pheasant weather is highly variable. I have hunted pheasants in the bedazzled sunlight found in Robert Abbett paintings. Some of the eeriest hunts I've known took place in fog so thick it conjured up visions of the Hound of the Baskervilles. On occasion I have chased roosters in air so sultry my partners and I were obliged to run the air conditioner when driving from field to field. But those days were oddities, not the usual thing. The usual thing is a sky the color of steel wool and a wind out of Saskatchewan that cuts through a hunter's coat like a knife.

I remember a December hunt in Iowa after a blizzard. The storm deposited banks of snow that mounded as high as our armpits. At times we got hopelessly stuck in the deep powder and could only escape by lying flat and rolling to freedom over the tops of the drifts.

Other hunts were memorable for winds that snatched the caps from our heads. On several occasions I have hunted in winds that rushed over the land with the force of a river in flood. A man can lean into a wind like that without falling down. When birds flush in a tempest, the hunter knows exactly which way they will fly. That would seem to make the shooting easy, but few hunters can swing a shotgun briskly enough to get a lead on a rooster riding a fifty-mile-an-hour gale.

Last December, my friends and I hunted in wind chills the television meteorologists described as "life-threatening." With our heads swathed in scarves and ice-fishing face masks, we looked more like *mujahadeen* than upland sportsmen. My partners sacrificed some tender skin during that hunt because their lips kept freezing to their metal dog whistles.

Another key element of pheasant hunting is the peculiar landscape of the pheasant, peculiar in part because so much of it is manmade.

The natural habitat of most upland birds is land that at least looks natural and pristine. Prairie grouse are found in fields of windswept grass that stretch from the foreground to the vanishing point. Ruffed grouse and woodcock flush from mazes of lacy timber common to second-growth forests. Although man has altered those landscapes, his handiwork is disguised. The hunter can imagine the cover he moves through is wild and natural.

A Brittany works a South Dakota field for late-season roosters. *Dale C. Spartas*

THE PAYOFF FOR HARD WORK: A PERFECT DELIVERY TO HAND. *Dale C. Spartas*

BROODING SKIES OVER A MIDWESTERN CORN FIELD. *Sherm Spoelstra*

DESERTED FARMSTEAD IN COLORADO. *Sherm Spoelstra*

But pheasants dwell in a special zone between the tame and the wild, between places that are manmade and places that are so disagreeable that nobody but a pheasant hunter would enter them. It is rare, when hunting pheasants, to be out of sight of something connected to civilization.

This in no way means that pheasant cover is tame. I have hunted pheasants in the stinking mud of marshes where the flag-topped phragmites stood higher above my head than my gun barrels would reach. Gun-wise roosters often hang out in woolly tangles of weeds where a pheasant flushing ten yards away might be screened from view. In a particularly dense South Dakota marsh, I tipped over to see if I could fall all the way down. I couldn't. The river bulrushes and cattails had grown up packed so tightly they held my body almost upright.

Pheasant cover can be big or small, complex or simple. My preferences are strongly for the large and complex. There are places where I can kill pheasants that I choose not to hunt because the cover is confining and dull. The larger and more varied the cover, the more complex and intriguing the hunt can be.

Many of the places we hunt pheasants are beautiful. I recently hunted an abandoned farm in western North Dakota where all the colors were sun-bleached and delicate. A sparkling blue river wound a sinuous path between shapely hills and out through a valley. The old farm buildings had weathered until they fitted the natural landscape as much as the buckbrush and plum thickets growing there. In Iowa I once followed a madly bouncing springer spaniel through a field of foxtail backlit by the setting sun, and when the rooster finally surged up from those golden weeds I thought I had never seen anything so lovely. In Minnesota, I hunted a large marsh right after a hoarfrost had coated each cattail with ice crystals that sparkled in the sun like flakes of mica.

Another peculiarity of pheasant hunting is the fact that the best of it takes place on private land.

In a perfect world, that land belongs to someone the hunter considers a friend, giving the hunt a conviviality that is unique in upland hunting. When farmers and hunters are old acquaintances, extra time must be allocated before the hunt for socializing. The hunter kicks his boots off in the mud room and pads around the kitchen in stocking feet, exchanging small talk about Lynette's piano lessons and how queer the weather has been.

Alas, few modern pheasant hunters know the luxury of hunting land owned by friends. Regional bird populations rise and fall, forcing hunters to drive great distances into new country to chase rumors of bird abundance. Those rumors often recede coyly before us like rainbows after a storm, but chase them we must.

THE END OF A GOLDEN RETRIEVER PUP'S FIRST DAY
IN THE FIELD. *Frank Oberle*

SOLITARY ROOSTER IN A MISSOURI CORN FIELD. *Denver Bryan*

FALLOW LAND, SUCH AS THIS FIELD IN KANSAS RETIRED UNDER THE FEDERAL CONSERVATION RESERVE PROGRAM (CRP), IS A BOON TO THE RING-NECKED PHEASANT. *Mike Blair*

A GOOD DOG, A GOOD GUN, AND A ROOSTER—THE STUFF GREAT MEMORIES ARE MADE OF.
Dale C. Spartas

To gain rights to hunt private land, therefore, the modern hunter must often go hat-in-hand to the back door of farmhouses to conduct a delicate social transaction with a stranger. These encounters are frequently bizarre because they thrust together people from social worlds that would otherwise never impinge upon each other.

Example: a man who owns several shopping centers approaches a farmer in a feedlot to make his pitch for hunting permission. The hunter, wearing British wax green hunting garb, stands ankle-deep in cow shit and adopts an expression he thinks will make him look like a nice and normal man. The bemused audience for this performance is a portly fellow in coveralls, a fraying jacket from Fleet Farm, and a sweat-stained cap promoting DeKalb hybrids. Should the hunter overplay his hand by admiring "the way those DeKalb hogs gain weight," the farmer might send him packing. Or he might not. The Good Lord never made a more earnest, hard-working or generous soul than the typical farmer in pheasant country.

I have approached strangers this way many, many times. Farm wives have shared coffee, lemonade, pies, and cookies with me. A few have trusted me enough to discuss the deprivations and sorrows of their isolated lives. With farmers I have discussed the weather, crop prices, the weather, politics, the weather, and pheasants. With sly indirection, farmers have often poked fun at me, and I sometimes didn't realize my leg had been pulled until hours later.

Let us sum up. Pheasant hunting derives its unique flavor from pheasant weather, from the rural landscape, and from the unusual social situation that brings together the hunter with rural families. All of which is true . . . and peripheral. What makes pheasant hunting so unique is the pheasant.

What a bird this is! Cocky and subtle. Smart and rugged. Explosive and fugitive. Clever, resourceful, and elusive. Courageous, wily, brassy, and unpredictable. And beautiful, too damned beautiful for words.

When Mother Nature designed the rooster pheasant, she indulged in a flight of whimsy. "I'm going to let it all hang out with this one," she said. "Let's see how many different colors I can load on one bird without making the thing look goofy or garish." The answer, by my count, is thirteen; thirteen wild and crazy colors, some straight, some iridescent. In my lifetime, several pheasants have escaped me because I was too awestruck by their beauty to bring my gun into action.

The inexperienced pheasant hunter, knowing the rooster pheasant is three feet long and decorated with more gaudy colors than can be found in a box

EVENING LIGHT CASTS A WARM GLOW ON A ROOSTER
IN AN IOWA CORN FIELD. *Roger A. Hill*

A FLOCK LOAFS ALONG A FENCEROW IN IOWA. *Roger A. Hill*

At the edge of a field in Iowa. *Roger A. Hill*

of Crayolas, expects this bird to stick out from its surroundings like a neon sign. Imagine how startled the beginner is, then, when a cock pheasant erupts from three inches of grass and slashes his way into the air, hurling throbbing curses and dumping gobs of whitewash to show his contempt. The beginner then blasts three ragged holes in the air.

Last winter I stood in a long, low shed and peered through dim light at a marvelous spectacle. About two hundred rooster pheasants milled in a circle around the shed like a giant school of fish. Beside me stood the man who had raised these birds and who fed them every day. I wondered if these birds would shy away from me, the stranger, and seek comfort from the man they knew best.

I was not prepared for what I saw. The roosters ignored me. As expected, they sought out the man who fed them . . . and did their best to kill him. Cock after cock rushed the keeper, leaped high and tried to slice his face with its spurs. Had that bunch of pheasants acquired a hand grenade, the results would not have been pretty. Those birds would have blown themselves up if they'd been sure of getting the farmer, too.

There never has been a tame pheasant. It isn't so with all upland birds. Quail are so trusting and comfortable with people that I've known hunters to give up quail hunting on just those grounds. The occasional ruffed grouse or turkey allows itself to become a pet. Worst of all, for me, is the woodcock. Even after I've missed them with two loads of number 8 shot, woodcock fail to understand that I'm out there to kill them. They land innocently a few feet away and wait for me to come flush (and miss) them again.

Nobody can say that about pheasants. *They know.* While young pheasants aren't born knowing about pheasant hunters, they quickly put it together every year. Gun-wise roosters know what hunters intend, how they act, and how to make them look like dunces. Experienced birds know what dogs can do and how to deal with them. I am even convinced that hard-hunted pheasants work out a pretty clear idea of what a shotgun can and cannot do. Perhaps the most important concept for understanding pheasant behavior in fall is the fact that *roosters learn the game.*

It simply takes a little experience. Before a young rooster has his first contact with hunters, he is as wary as any other upland bird—no more, no less. That is, if a hunter gets too close, the young rooster might skulk, sneak, run, or flush to safety. But if that pheasant survives his first brush with hunters, he will never again be quite so easy to approach and flush in range. And if that cock survives several contacts with hunters, he becomes a consummate tactician. He

A ROOSTER HEADS FOR SAFETY. *Dale C. Spartas*

A HUNTER SWINGS ON A FLUSHING ROOSTER. *Denver Bryan*

SITTING TIGHT. *Gary R. Zahm*

becomes a pheasant.

The gun-wise rooster is mobile and unpredictable. He appears where least expected and disappears like smoke. He might choose bold tactics to avoid detection, or he might play it cute. The only consistent thing about him is that he will usually do what the hunter least expects or wants.

If you want him to sit, he'll run. If you want him to run East, he'll go North, South, or West. If you want him to move toward a line of blockers, he'll sneak back between two of the drivers. If you hope he will stay on the ground long enough to let you catch up with him, he'll flush wild. If you want him to flush, he'll refuse to fly, even to the point of letting a Labrador seize him in its slavering jaws.

If you surround a pocket marsh with hunters on three sides and all rush in at the same moment, which way do you suppose the birds will fly? The answer is obvious to any veteran hunter. The pheasants—or at least the roosters—will fly out the fourth direction, leaving by the one exit not covered with a gun.

If you put up a flock of five pheasants, four of which are hens, guess which four birds will appear in shotgun range? Guess which bird will flush on the far side of the flock, just beyond the reach of your barrels?

If you hunt cautiously, the pheasants are apt to boil up out of the cover while you are still far behind them. Yet if you hunt at the gallop, sprinting to keep near the birds you know are dashing ahead of you, some roosters will lie low to let you pass. Others will flush raucously behind you, cackling derisively as they sail toward the center of a marsh where you'll never see them again.

What makes pheasant hunting so special is the pheasant himself, and he offers no quarter. He'll outrun you or outmaneuver you. He'll squirt down a woodchuck hole or wade into a creek to throw you off his trail. He'll crawl under a brush pile or dash to safety in plain sight across a plowed field. He'll beat you with speed, with caution, or with cunning. Sometimes he beats you with sheer nerve, like the poker player who bluffs his way to the biggest pot of the evening with nothing more in his hand than a Jack high card. Like a great chess player, he always thinks several moves ahead.

Pheasants would be too difficult to hunt if they all started the season as canny as they become by season's end. But they do not. Each season begins with a fresh supply of uneducated cocks. Early in the season, the hunter can go afield with the fair expectation of shooting a daily limit of roosters. But as the season winds on, the game gets tougher day by day. By the bitter end of the season, the roosters are so smart it is a rare accident when one is trapped into flushing anywhere near a hunter. Late season

A SNOW-COVERED CORN FIELD IN MINNESOTA PROVIDES SAFE HAVEN FOR THIS ROOSTER.
Daniel J. Cox

Two Ringnecks play a high-stakes game of hide-and-seek with a hunter. *Judd Cooney*

COTTONWOOD GROVES PROVIDE EXCELLENT HUNTING GROUNDS
FOR WESTERN MONTANA RINGNECKS. *Dale C. Spartas*

"Don't shoot—hen!" *Dale C. Spartas*

roosters will make you cry in your beer, tear your hair, and say all the bad words you know.

Above all, this is what makes pheasant hunting so distinctive. Pheasants don't run around with maps, compasses, and guidebooks about hunter tactics. They just behave as if they understood and used such aids. Experienced pheasants present tactical and strategic challenges that are unlike those posed by any other upland bird.

Beginning hunters savor the wild action and easy shots typical of opening weekend hunts. I know hunters who pursue opening weekend pheasants and no others. Because pheasant seasons open on different weekends in different states, these hunters drive from state to state to take advantage of all the naive pheasants they can bag by hunting many opening weekends. When there are no more season openings available, these hunters either case their guns or renounce wild birds in favor of game farm pheasants. To put this in less kind terms, these fellows are afraid of smart pheasants.

Experienced hunters often follow an entirely different program. Many veteran pheasant hunters stay home on opening weekend, in part because there are so many boorish hunters afield. But they also bypass the easy action because opening weekend pheasants simply aren't as interesting to hunt as birds that have had some experience with hunters.

Opening weekend pheasants are *good* game birds but experienced pheasants are *great* game birds. One bird is pleasant to hunt. The other is one of the world's most challenging game birds. The opening weekend bird can usually be bagged with a modest amount of luck and effort. Effort and luck count for little when the roosters have learned about hunters. To be successful with veteran cocks, the hunter will need effort, and luck—and considerable skill.

And help—a lot of help—from a well-trained pheasant dog.

Much of the distinctive flavor of pheasant hunting arises from the distinctive work of a good pheasant dog. A veteran dog will work pheasants with specialized tactics he doesn't use on other birds. He really has no choice. Experienced pheasants don't behave like other birds. They require special handling because they are so tricky and variable.

A good pheasant dog knows there is no single right way to hunt pheasants. There are times to hunt cautiously and times to drive hard. Highly trained dogs that obey commands like little robots rarely make good pheasant dogs because they cannot adjust to all the different evasion tactics used by some roosters. A good pheasant dog thinks for itself rather than blindly obeying commands. Good pheasant dogs obey their masters to the extent they can, but keep their eyes on the prize: that intoxicatingly

A WELL-TRAINED LAB. *Dale C. Spartas*

WITH MUSCLES QUIVERING, AN ENGLISH POINTER STANDS ON POINT! *Denver Bryan*

smelly bird in the weeds.

According to the old wives' tale, pheasants can ruin dogs by refusing to play the game by ordinary polite rules observed by most upland birds. Actually, the opposite is true. It probably is true that pheasants can cause stupid or high-strung dogs to run amok. But a *good* dog—a dog with enough natural ability and manners—only becomes better by hunting pheasants. He'll experience his share of frustration and defeat, but the good dog will eventually learn the ways of gun-wise roosters and learn what he can do about them. Pheasants don't ruin good dogs; they turn good dogs into great dogs.

It doesn't happen overnight. Young dogs, sensing that the pheasants are running, will increase their own speed in order to keep up. The result is often a bird boosted into the sky out of range. Veteran pheasant dogs have little use for speed. They rely upon scent and their accumulated knowledge of pheasant behavior to work out the trail. It is a joy to watch a smart old pheasant dog in action; you can almost see the wheels turning in his head as he combines fresh scent with old experience to find a tricky bird.

Dog and man form a team. The man is painfully awkward and slow. His sense of smell is worthless and he has lost most of the natural instincts of a predator. But he has a brain, which is occasionally handy, and he has a shotgun, which becomes very handy when birds flush. The dog is a wonderful athlete who has a nose that can interpret the shifting plumes of scent left in the grass by the birds. Although the dog eats commercial chow and sleeps on his master's couch, he is still a predator. His blood sings with the joy of the hunt.

These two are rather eccentric partners, yet each supplies what the other lacks. With enough time and experience, the dog-and-man team learns the ways of pheasants and learns how to function as a team. Even then, many birds will beat them. Which is as it should be. In the dramatic contest we call pheasant hunting, the team of one good man and one good dog will need to perform at a high level to prevail over the wiliness of one good pheasant.

Pheasant hunting can take many forms. At its lowest, it takes the form of a man stepping out of his pickup to blast a bird in a ditch. It often takes the form of group drives involving a few hunters or a great many. The sport has early and late season forms. Some forms involve dogs and some do not.

But I believe the essence of pheasant hunting—certainly the most elegant and fascinating form it takes—is represented by the situation just described: one hunter, one dog, one bird. Ideally, each of these will have enough prior experience to know the game.

Let the hunt take place sometime near the

PRAISE FOR A JOB WELL-DONE. *Dale C. Spartas*

middle of the season. The weather will have an edge to it, but won't be brutal. The field should be large and complex enough to allow for many possibilities. And since we are talking about an ideal situation, let's illuminate that field with the golden light of a late afternoon in November.

What you have in this situation are all the elements needed to create one of the most beautiful, exciting, and challenging upland bird hunts in the world. When the bird eludes the man-dog hunting team, as most do, the hunters should feel no shame. They were beaten fairly by a great game bird. When the hunters succeed, they can take pride in what they have accomplished. They didn't just shoot a bird, they proved themselves the equal of a *pheasant!*

A PERFECT END TO A PERFECT DAY.
Dale C. Spartas

SPRING'S NEW GREEN AND RINGNECK ROOSTER IN OREGON'S VAST GRASSLANDS. *Tom & Pat Leeson*

A HUNTER AND A GERMAN WIREHAIR WORK A FARMSTEAD FOR PHEASANTS. *Dale C. Spartas*

A RETRIEVE FROM A CRP FIELD. *Dale C. Spartas*

LIGHT FADES AS A HUNTER-DOG TEAM WORKS A MISSOURI FARM. *Denver Bryan*

Denver Bryan

WHEN ONE HUNTS WITH A FRIEND, IT HARDLY MATTERS WHO KILLS

THE BIRDS. IT HARDLY MATTERS WHETHER BIRDS ARE KILLED AT ALL.

ONE MUST DO RIGHT BY THE BIRDS, BY ONE'S PARTNER, AND BY

THE DOGS. HUNTING IS A PATH, A MUDDY, BRUSHY, DANK, AND

SPOOR-WRITTEN PATH ALONG WHICH THE SEEKER, IF HIS SPIRIT BE

RIGHT, CAN TRULY FEEL THE EARTH. IF HE IS FORTUNATE, HE

TRAVELS WITH A TRUE DOG AND A TRUE FRIEND.

Charles Fergus, *A Rough-Shooting Dog*

HUNTERS AND DOGS TAKE A MOMENT BEFORE WORKING THE LAST FIELD OF THE DAY.
Dale C. Spartas

ROOSTER TAKES FLIGHT; HUNTER TAKES AIM. *Judd Cooney*

IF YOU ARE SERIOUS ABOUT LEARNING THIS GRAND SPORT, BUY THE BEST DOG YOU CAN AFFORD AND THREE PAIRS OF NYLON-FACED HUNTING PANTS. TRAIN YOUR DOG OR PUT HIM IN THE HANDS OF SOMEONE WHO CAN. THEN GO TO THE BIRDIEST, WEEDIEST SPOTS YOU KNOW AND PUT THE DOG DOWN. WALK BEHIND HIM, LISTEN WITH CARE TO WHAT HE TELLS YOU ABOUT PHEASANTS. HUNT UNTIL YOUR PANTS HAVE BOBWIRE CUTS IN THE CROTCH AND CUFFS FRAYED UNTIL THEY HOLD COCKLEBURS LIKE A SPRINGER'S SILKY EARS. WHEN ALL YOUR PANTS ARE TOO HOLEY TO BE WORN IN THE PRESENCE OF LADIES, YOUR DOG WILL HAVE TOLD YOU MOST OF WHAT YOU WILL EVER KNOW ABOUT PHEASANT HUNTING.

Steve Grooms, *Pheasant Hunter's Harvest*

A PROUD YELLOW LABRADOR WITH A RINGNECK.
Denver Bryan

HOLDING TIGHT—ONE OF MANY TACTICS IN THE RINGNECK'S BAG OF TRICKS. *Dale C. Spartas*

A ROOSTER SITS TIGHT UNDER THE NOSE OF AN ENGLISH POINTER. *Dale C. Spartas*

A ring-necked pheasant in Wisconsin. *John R. Ford*

He's a survivor. To the gunner his golden hues are as major a part of the autumn colors of our country as the oak and maple. I like to watch him strut and cock an eye at me—from sixty yards away, of course—saying, "Catch me if you can!" And, more often than not by a lot, I don't . . . which is absolutely fine by me.

Gene Hill, *A Gallery of Waterfowl and Upland Birds*

SEASONS COME AND GO, BUT THE MEMORIES LAST A LIFETIME. *Dale C. Spartas*

SNOW FALLS ON A PHEASANT HEN ON A GRAY
WINTER DAY IN MINNESOTA.
Daniel J. Cox

SURVIVAL FOR THIS ROOSTER MEANS FINDING FOOD IN A SNOW-COVERED IOWA CORN FIELD.
Roger A. Hill

A PHEASANT ROOSTER WITH PUFFED PLUMAGE TRIES TO STAY WARM
ON A COLD MINNESOTA MORNING. *Daniel J. Cox*

THE REWARDS FROM A DAY AFIELD. *Dale C. Spartas*

LEFT: A MIXED DOUBLE TO START THE DAY. *Dale C. Spartas*

For the hunter, fall is the island and the rest of the
year is the swim. The fine untroubled October days, the
leaves falling in earnest, the colors transferring
themselves to the ground, reflecting upward toward the
half-clad trees in a subtle, short-lived glow, the coverts
opening up, shooting becoming practicable at last.

Charles Fergus, *A Rough-Shooting Dog*

Pheasant hunters discuss last-minute tactics in the fading sunlight
of a November day in Minnesota. *Denver Bryan*

A ROOSTER PAUSES—WYOMING. *D. Robert Franz*

NOW YOU SEE ME, NOW YOU DON'T: A TYPICAL PHEASANT MANEUVER.
Tom & Pat Leeson

A CLASSIC POINT. *Dale C. Spartas*

*T*O BE OUT ON THE LAND IN
ALL WEATHERS, THE GUN BARRELS WARM
IN THE SUN OR SHELVED WITH SNOW OR
BEADED WITH RAIN, THE LIGHT WAN OR
BLAZING, THE WIND RATTLING LEAVES DOWN
THE HOLLOW THAT YESTERDAY BRIMMED
WITH FOG; TO BE OUT AMONG STONES AND
TREES AND STREAMS, AMONG THE ANIMALS
WHO RESIDE HERE DAY IN AND DAY OUT . . .
TO BE OUT ON THE LAND WITH A SILENT
COMPANION WHOSE BOUNDLESS,
INSTINCTIVE ENERGY CLARIFIES AND
INTENSIFIES ONE'S OWN; TO LISTEN AS FALL
SEGUES INTO WINTER, TO WALK UPON ONE
SHORT SEGMENT OF THE EVER-REPEATING
CYCLE; TO COME HOME FULLY SPENT, EMPTY-
HANDED OR BEARING FOOD FOR THE TABLE;
TO SIT BY THE FIRE AND FEEL THE DAY DYING
DOWN: THIS IS WHAT IT IS TO HUNT. THIS
IS WHAT IT IS TO LIVE.

―⟜═ ═⟞―

Charles Fergus, *A Rough-Shooting Dog*

PHEASANT HUNTING IS SHARING
A GLORIOUS SUNSET WITH YOUR BEST
FRIENDS AND HONORING THE BIRD FOR
THE CHALLENGE IT PROVIDES.
Denver Bryan

by Russ Sewell & Dave Nomsen

THE RINGNECK IN NORTH AMERICA: A BRIEF HISTORY

The life of the ring-necked pheasant in North America is interwoven with the stories and lives of American hunters and farmers. By the time pheasants arrived on this continent in the late nineteenth century, the landscape of America had already changed to a mosaic of small farms, wetlands, prairie, and woods. Vast acreages of swaying prairie grass had given way to

the advance of settlers and the horse and plow. Unable to adapt to the loss of prairie, the populations of native wildfowl, such as sharp-tailed grouse, dwindled, and the overall abundance of wildlife diminished. Wildfowl hunters called for a sporting gamebird that would be self-propagating, pleasing to the palate, and able to thrive in close association with agriculture.

A COCK SCRATCHES FOR FOOD AT THE EDGE OF A
PHEASANTS FOREVER MANAGEMENT AREA.
Roger A. Hill

COVERING THE FLUSH. *Mike Blair*

This call was heeded in 1882 when the U.S. consul-general to Shanghai, Judge Owen Denny, imported approximately fifty pheasants to his home in the Willamette Valley of Oregon. Although this was not the first introduction attempt, it was the first of any significance to establish birds in the wild. A decade later the so-called Denny birds had multiplied to the extent that Oregon held its first pheasant hunting season. An estimated fifty thousand birds were harvested on opening day—testimony to the pheasant's prolific nature and ability to thrive in the new agricultural landscape.

As word spread, every state in the nation wanted pheasants, and birds were imported from the farthest reaches of Europe and Asia. Today's ringneck typifies the melting pot phenomenon; it is the descendant of thirteen subspecies that met and interbred in America. Pheasants flourished in the northern half of the United States and the southern reaches of the Canadian provinces. The corn and alfalfa fields, fencerows, and grassy areas of the Midwest proved to be prime habitat; the crops of the southern states did not suit the beautiful birds.

The ringneck's ability to evade, outwit, and fluster hunters and their dogs quickly established it as a worthy quarry among American sportsmen and women. Every farm boy who could hoard enough money from his trapline to order a shotgun from Sears walked the corn stubble in search of a ringneck cock to grace Sunday's dinner table. Pheasant hunting became an inheritance shared between generations.

The Second World War removed almost an entire generation of American hunters from the family farm. As a result, during the war years, pheasant populations peaked in many midwestern states. Wildlife biologists working in the newly founded field of wildlife management documented fall populations as high as four hundred birds per square mile of land. When the war finally ended, many soldiers and factory workers did not return to the farm, settling instead in cities and suburbs. The rural culture of small farms and towns closely tied to the land would not return.

The end of the war brought burgeoning population growth. In response, the government encouraged farmers to drain wetlands, remove fencerows, and apply pesticides and fertilizers in the quest for increased production. Farmers switched from raising livestock and multiple crops to businesses devoted entirely to producing a single crop, with farm machinery designed to produce larger crops with less labor. Agribusiness grew, as small family farms—and the habitat best suited to pheasants—continued to disappear. Ringneck populations began to dwindle.

STUBBLE FIELDS NEXT TO BRUSHY COVER: PRIME WINTER HABITAT FOR RINGNECKS AND HUNGARIAN PARTRIDGE. *Dale C. Spartas*

IT'S BEEN SAID THAT A PHEASANT'S BEST DEFENSE IS THE RUCKUS IT MAKES WHILE TAKING FLIGHT.
Denver Bryan

By the mid 1950s, however, pheasant numbers were on the rebound. The reasons for this renaissance lay, oddly enough, with the federal government and its relations with the nation's farmers. Government intervention in farming prior to the 1930s had been minimal. The ensuing six decades revealed that federal agricultural policies can have a dramatic effect on pheasant populations.

In 1956 the United States Department of Agriculture (USDA) initiated the Soil Bank Program, which included a Conservation Reserve (CR) provision that retired nearly 28 million acres by 1960. This long-term land retirement program designed to reduce commodity surpluses proved a godsend for pheasants and those who hunt them. Pheasant populations peaked at near-record levels in response to grass and legume cover plantings required under the CR provision. Each fall small towns bustled with the invasion of hunters, providing a much-needed boost to rural economies. However, by the late 1960s, all CR contracts had expired, and the CR wildlife-producing acreages were tilled once again into crop production. This loss of habitat caused pheasant numbers to plummet, and hunters were left to lament and reminisce about the "good old days."

More recently, pheasant populations have risen two- and three-fold due to increased habitat resulting from the passage of the Conservation Reserve Program (CRP) of 1985 and 1990. Designed as a commodity reduction program, CRP has idled nearly 38 million acres of marginal farmlands, improving soil and water conservation and benefiting wildlife. Even species such as prairie chicken and sharp-tailed grouse, which require extensive blocks of grassland, have responded favorably.

Though ringneck populations have rebounded, the story is not over. Many CRP contracts are nearing expiration, and Congress is once again debating the necessity of a long-term land retirement program. Without acres reserved from cropping that pheasants can use as nesting cover and protective shelter, their future is uncertain. Conservationists in concert with many farmers and agriculture representatives are lobbying for a continuation of CRP. In 1995 USDA did extend some CRP contracts, but it remains to be seen whether hunters will once again have to look back fondly to the "good old days."

The ringneck has proven itself a survivor, but with a little help, it can thrive in America's intensively cultivated farmlands. This extraordinary bird will continue to serve as a barometer of the land's health, from which we can judge the success or failure of our stewardship.

A ROOSTER SEEKS COVER. *Dale C. Spartas*

by Russ Sewell

A Year in the Life: The Ringneck's Natural History

The ringneck's fight for survival begins with spring's lengthening daylight and warming temperatures. Wintering flocks of roosters and hens disband as the greening of the landscape gradually spreads over farm country. Dominant roosters, adorned with enlarged crimson wattles, challenge

lesser males in pitched battles to establish crowing territories. Victorious cocks win the right to court and breed any hen traveling through their bailiwicks. Roosters lure as many hens as possible into a "harem." A single rooster has been known to gather groups of up to fifteen or more hens. The normal rooster's harem, though, contains two to three hens.

The well-camouflaged brown hens, smaller in size than their mates, move freely through established crowing

Cock bird in mating display.
Tom & Pat Leeson

RITES OF SPRING: RINGNECK COCK AND HEN DURING MATING RITUAL. *Tom & Pat Leeson*

territories. At each hen's approach the rooster conducts an elaborate display of his plumage. Roosters are almost thirty inches in length, of which twenty inches is tail, and possess iridescent plumage of incredible colors. The rooster—with head lowered, wings and tail spread, and body positioned sideways—makes his best proposal to the hen. This colorful ceremonial display inflates a two- to-three pound adult rooster into a figure three times that size. As if this show of spring finery was not lure enough, roosters also woo hens with soft clucks and purrs.

Courtship, nesting, and breeding continue throughout April and peak in early May. A brief interlude of mating produces eggs that are fertile for up to forty days. For pheasant hens to develop eggs, their diet must be high in calcium. The hens acquire this from grit, the abrasive material (i.e. limestone gravel) eaten with their food and used in the gizzard for digestive purposes.

To nest, pheasant hens seek out areas of grassy cover. Early in the season, grasses that have withstood winter's snows, such as switchgrass and big bluestem, are ideal. Later, nesting hens choose sites in alfalfa fields and other areas of plush greenery. The nest is constructed by scratching out a shallow depression and lining it with grass and leaves.

With construction complete, the hen lays one egg approximately every thirty hours for a clutch of approximately ten eggs. She then adds an extra lining of breast feathers to the nest and begins the incubation process. Delaying incubation until the entire clutch is assembled ensures the timely hatching of chicks. Over a period of twenty-two to twenty-three days, the hen diligently sits on her clutch, guarding it from egg-eating predators such as skunks and raccoons. If the nest is located in an alfalfa field, the hen must also contend with high-speed mowing operations. Because of the development of early-maturing varieties of alfalfa, mowing often conflicts with pheasant nesting, and countless nests, as well as hens, perish beneath the blades of hay mowers. Mother Nature can also foil the hen's efforts with drenching storms and extreme temperature fluctuations that may destroy the nest and eggs.

Fortunately pheasant hens are persistent re-nesters; if the initial effort fails, they will make several attempts at producing a successful hatch. However each nesting attempt is an additional physical burden upon the hen and produces less chicks than if the initial attempt succeeded. During incubation, hens leave their nests only occasionally for a quick meal. Roosters share little in parental responsibilities. Instead, they maintain their territories and attend to other hens within their

PHEASANT HEN ON NEST. *Judd Cooney*

THE CYCLE BEGINS ONCE AGAIN. *Richard Day*

harems throughout the spring.

Hatching usually occurs in mid-June. Life for pheasant chicks begins with the pipping of the eggshell. Within twenty-four hours all of the chicks hatch, emerging fully clothed in down and ready to forage for food. Pheasant hens and their broods spend the first few weeks in close proximity to the nesting area. A typical day for a brood consists of early mornings spent along roadsides or in open areas where the dew hangs heavy on plants, providing water to quench the birds' thirst. Mid-morning the hen and her chicks move to medium-height grass and forb cover, where insects abound. With their fill of insects, the brood heads to dense grass cover to loaf during midday. Evening finds the brood roosting in uncut grass or weed cover from the previous year. Although adult pheasants are omnivorous, chicks consume such insects as grasshoppers, ants, and crickets exclusively for the first few weeks of life.

Within two weeks after hatching, pheasant chicks develop the feathers necessary to take short flights. After six or seven weeks, they shed their downy covering, which is replaced by juvenile feathers. Despite a close watch by the hen, over a fourth of the chicks are lost to predators before reaching eight weeks of age. During the eighth week, pheasant hens abandon their young, having taught them the skills required for survival. By eighteen weeks, juveniles can only be distinguished from adult birds by a trained eye.

Nesting and raising a brood is not easy for the hen pheasant, and she must work especially hard to restore her physical well-being before winter. Even with an abundance of food during the summer and early autumn, hens that begin nesting in poor physical condition often perish. As a species, pheasants are prolific but short-lived. Autumn flocks usually contain seventy percent fledglings and thirty percent adults, with the majority of the adults being less than two years old.

During late summer pheasants feed upon the succulent vegetation, grain waste, berries, weed seeds, and insects common in farm country. Autumn's arrival spurs an increase in feeding to build the fat reserves necessary to survive winter.

In the fall pheasants begin feeding shortly before sunrise, returning to loaf in cover by mid-morning. Pheasants spend a good portion of their day preening and dusting in the protection of farmland shelterbelts and thickets. Dusting, the act of fluffing dirt into the feathers, helps rid the birds of parasites. By late afternoon the birds return to the grain fields, foraging heavily on protein-rich grains remaining after harvest. Evening finds the birds roosting in the cattails and sedges of wetlands, or in the dense rank

P HEASANT HEN AND CHICK. *Alan & Sandy Carey*

THE BUFF, BLACK, AND CREAM PLUMAGE OF THE PHEASANT HEN CAN
RENDER HER NEARLY INVISIBLE. *Judd Cooney*

ROOSTER PHEASANT IN GLORIOUS COLOR. *Judd Cooney*

81

grasses in odd areas of tillage, roadsides, or land idled by government farm programs.

With the onslaught of winter, when wetlands and other areas of herbaceous cover are buried in snow, pheasants are forced to rely on less-available woody cover for protection from the cold. If food resources are not located close to shelterbelts, woods, and understory shrubs, birds become dangerously exposed to both weather and predators. During severe winters, pheasants often segregate into flocks by gender. During winter's short days the birds feed voraciously on the grain remaining from harvest, as well as on the seeds and fruits of weeds. Birds fortunate enough to find adequate habitat, survive extreme weather conditions, and evade hunters and predators live to pass on their savvy to their young the following spring.

FOOD RESOURCES, SUCH AS THIS CORN FIELD
IN KANSAS, ARE ONE OF THE KEYS TO
ENSURING THE RINGNECK'S SURVIVAL.
Frank Oberle

A HUNTER SALLIES FORTH IN PURSUIT OF PHEASANTS AND SOMETIMES FINDS THEM AND SOMETIMES DOES NOT. AT THE TIME, HE THINKS THE FINDING IS WHAT MATTERS. LATER HE LOOKS BACK OVER IT ALL AND SEES THAT THE MAGIC OF THE SPORT CONSISTS OF ALL THE OTHER THINGS HE FOUND WHILE TRYING TO FIND PHEASANTS. THEY ARE THE TRUE PHEASANT HUNTER'S HARVEST.

―――◦◦―――

Steve Grooms, *Pheasant Hunter's Harvest*

DOGS AND HUNTER PURSUE PRAIRIE RINGNECKS
IN CENTRAL MONTANA. *Denver Bryan*

A HUNTER BAGS A ROOSTER.
Dale C. Spartas

HUNTING ROOSTERS UNDER A PRAIRIE SKY. *Dale C. Spartas*

DOG ON POINT, GUN AT THE READY, ANTICIPATION OF THE FLUSH.
Alan & Sandy Carey

A ROOSTER BASKS IN THE AFTERNOON SUN.
Tom & Pat Leeson

ROOSTER AND SPANISH SIDELOCK.
Dale C. Spartas

*N*OWHERE IS THE WIZARD AMONG GAME BIRDS MORE AT HOME THAN ON THE ROLLING PRAIRIES, WHERE HE CAN STRETCH HIS LEGS—AND YOURS—TO THE NEXT HORIZON. HE SAYS, SIMPLY, "CATCH ME IF YOU CAN," AND SOMETIMES WE DO— BUT NOT ENOUGH TIMES TO TAKE THE LUSTER FROM THE THRILL.

⟢⟝⟞⟢

Dale C. Spartas, in *Game & Gun*

A HUSBAND AND WIFE WORK THE GRASSLANDS.
Ben O. Williams

LATE-SEASON HUNTING MEANS WORKING CATTAILS AND BULRUSHES
FOR GUN-SMART ROOSTERS. *Denver Bryan*

IF YOU THINK ANY PHEASANT SHOT IS TOO EASY, WAIT A
COUPLE OF SECONDS. IT'LL GET SPORTIER BEFORE YOU CAN
DRAW TWO MORE BREATHS.

John Madson, *The Ring-Necked Pheasant*

RINGNECK ROOSTER EXPLODES FROM CATTAILS. *Denver Bryan*

THE ROOSTER GRABS ONTO THE WORLD WITH BOTH FEET AS IF SOMEONE WERE TRYING TO PULL IT AWAY FROM HIM FOREVER, STRETCHES MIGHTILY TOWARD HEAVEN, OPENS HIS MOUTH WIDE ENOUGH TO SWALLOW A GOLF BALL, AND LETS GO WITH A SQUAWK THAT SOUNDS LIKE A TON OF ANTHRACITE GOING DOWN A CHUTE INTO HELL. HE THEN FOLLOWS THIS EXHIBITION BY BEATING HIS WINGS AGAINST HIS BODY LIKE TARZAN CHALLENGING KING KONG. MAYBE I'M GETTING A BIT EXUBERANT HERE, BUT YOU GET THE IDEA. PHEASANTS AIN'T BASHFUL IN THE SPRING.

Bob Bell, *Hunting the Long-Tailed Bird*

PHEASANT ROOSTER IN FULL MATING DISPLAY.
Denver Bryan

A RINGNECK COCK PAUSES IN A FIELD OF GRASSES AND ARROWLEAF BALSAMROOT.
Tim Christie

BARLEY FOXTAIL WAVES IN THE PRAIRIE BREEZE. *Jeff Foott*

PHEASANT HEN IN CORN. *Roger A. Hill*

IOWA ROOSTER IN MORNING SUN. *Roger A. Hill*

STARTLED BY THE SUDDEN FLUSH OF A PHEASANT. *Ben O. Williams*

WILD PHEASANTS WERE CAGEY BIRDS
THAT RAN LIKE RACE HORSES AND DISAPPEARED
IN SPARSE NEARLY NONEXISTENT COVER PLAYING
THE NOW-YOU-SEE-ME NOW-YOU-DON'T GAME QUITE
EFFECTIVELY. HUNTING THEM REQUIRED MILITARY
MANEUVERS AND SLY OR DOWN-AND-DIRTY TACTICS.
THEY DID NOT CACKLE WHEN FLUSHED PRONOUNCING,
"I'M A COCK, I'M A COCK, SHOOT! SHOOT!" INSTEAD
THEY SLIPPED OUT QUIETLY AND LOW AT 25 TO 30
YARDS. THEY WERE FAST, TWICE AS FAST AS THEIR
PEN-RAISED COUSINS AND POSSIBLY FASTER THAN
A GROUSE. . . . WILD PHEASANTS HAVE MY RESPECT;
I LOVE HUNTING THEM FOR THEY ARE WORTHY
AND FORMIDABLE OPPONENTS.

Dale C. Spartas, in *The Double Gun Journal*

A PHEASANT HUNTER WORKS A FIELD OF STANDING CORN, SOUTH DAKOTA.
Daniel J. Cox

ENGLISH SETTER ON POINT. *Denver Bryan*

A Springer spaniel makes a snappy delivery. *Denver Bryan*

HEADING HOME. *Denver Bryan*

PASSING ON THE HERITAGE. *Dale C. Spartas*

PHEASANT HUNTING: A DEEP AND RICH TRADITION.
Dale C. Spartas

I HUNT FOR BEAUTY, FOR CHALLENGE, FOR FRIENDSHIP,
FOR THE JOY OF WORKING WITH A DOG, FOR THE DRAMA OF
THE ENCOUNTER, AND FOR THE SENSE OF ACCOMPLISHMENT
THAT FOLLOWS BY DOING IT RIGHT.

Steve Grooms, *Pheasant Hunter's Harvest*

With its metallic green and blue head, snow white neck band and multi-colored body, a cock pheasant is as breathtaking and beautiful as autumn leaves in peak foliage.

Dale C. Spartas, in *Gray's Sporting Journal*

Ringneck rooster's iridescent glory.
Denver Bryan

OPENING DAY. *Denver Bryan*

ORDINARILY I LEAVE THE ROOSTING
COVERS ALONE IN MY THEORY THAT A MAN'S HOUSE
IS HIS CASTLE AND THAT GOES FOR THE PHEASANTS AS
WELL, BUT THE OLD DOG IS SORT OF TWISTING MY ARM
AND REMINDING ME THAT THERE IS SOME TIME TO GO
BEFORE DARK. I TRY TO ARGUE WITH HER BUT IT'S NO
USE. SHE REMINDS ME THAT WE TOOK A BIRD OR TWO
THERE WHEN SHE WAS A PUPPY AND I TELL HER THAT
WAS TRAINING AND SHE SAYS THAT SHE'S OLD AND
CAN'T SEE OR HEAR TOO WELL ANYMORE AND HAS TO
MAKE DO. WE HEAD TOWARD THE LITTLE SWAMP, SHE
AT A TROT, LOOKING BACK TO MAKE SURE I'M THERE.

Gene Hill, *A Listening Walk—and Other Stories*

PHEASANT FLOCK IN WINTER. *Judd Cooney*

COCK PHEASANT TAKING REFUGE FROM WINTER WINDS ALONG A FENCEROW. *Judd Cooney*

*T*HE [FEDERAL FARM] PROGRAMS
AND PHEASANTS IN AMERICA ARE
INTERTWINED. THE LESSONS OF THE
PAST HAVE SHOWN US THAT SHORT-TERM
SET-ASIDES DO LITTLE FOR WILDLIFE,
PARTICULARLY PHEASANTS. LONG-TERM
LAND RETIREMENTS, HOWEVER, HAVE
PROVEN TO BE A BOON FOR RINGNECKS. . . .
AGRICULTURE AND WILDLIFE CAN
COHABIT, AND THERE IS VALUE TO A SOUND
ENVIRONMENT. AND PERHAPS THE PEOPLE
WHO RECOGNIZE THIS ARE OUR
GREATEST RESOURCE OF ALL.

Chris Dorsey, *Pheasant Days*

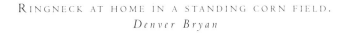

RINGNECK AT HOME IN A STANDING CORN FIELD.
Denver Bryan

by Dave Nomsen

PHEASANTS FOREVER: THE STORY

Since 1982, Pheasants Forever, Inc. (PF), the nation's largest nonprofit upland wildlife conservation organization, has been fighting to improve conditions for wildlife dependent upon America's farmlands. Pheasants Forever is dedicated to the protection and enhancement of pheasant and other wildlife populations in North America through habitat improvement, public awareness and education, and land management beneficial to farmers and wildlife alike.

Locally, PF chapters maintain control over habitat funds and work in cooperation with resource professionals, farmers, and landowners to establish habitat programs customized to meet wildlife needs in their area. Focusing on habitat improvements, chapters establish and maintain nesting cover and winter cover plantings, establish food plots, restore wetlands, and complete land acquisitions. Acquisitions are open to public hunting for sporting enthusiasts. Since inception, Pheasants Forever chapters have spent millions on habitat projects improving hundreds of thousands of acres. Pheasants Forever projects benefit more than pheasants and provide other wildlife with critical habitat, improve soil and water conservation, add aesthetic beauty, and increase recreational opportunities.

Pheasants Forever's commitment to ensuring our nation's hunting heritage and outdoor legacy is continued through public awareness and educational efforts. The innovative Kids For Pheasants program, the cornerstone of PF's conservation education emphasis, assists youth in learning about the shooting sports and the stewardship of our natural resources. Through PF publications, billboard campaigns, and other public awareness programs, Pheasants Forever focuses on today's and tomorrow's needs of wildlife.

Pheasants Forever supports conservation legislation benefiting the ringneck and other wildlife in federal and state legislative arenas. PF has been instrumental in developing and implementing state pheasant stamp habitat improvement programs, and promotes sound conservation policy in harmony with agriculture.

The accomplishments of dedicated Pheasants Forever volunteers, working in close cooperation with farmers, landowners, educators, and wildlife resource professionals, stand as a legacy and challenge to future generations to build upon. Working together we can make a difference for wildlife, and the future of pheasants and pheasant hunting has never looked brighter.

ACKNOWLEDGMENTS

The Publishers gratefully acknowledge the following sources:

Page 6
from *The Upland Gamehunter's Bible* by Dan Holland. Copyright 1961. Doubleday, New York.

Pages 45, 58, 63
from *A Rough-Shooting Dog* by Charles Fergus. Copyright 1991. Lyons & Burford, Publishers, New York.

Pages 48, 84, 107
from *Pheasant Hunter's Harvest* by Steve Grooms. Copyright 1990. Lyons & Burford, Publishers, New York.

Page 52
from *A Gallery of Waterfowl and Upland Birds* by Gene Hill. Copyright 1983 by Gene Hill, Safari Press, Huntington Beach, California.

Page 91
from "To Catch A Wizard" by Dale C. Spartas in *Game & Gun*, November/December, 1993.

Page 93
from *The Ring-Necked Pheasant* by John Madson. Copyright 1962. The Winchester Press, East Alton, Illinois.

Page 95
from *Hunting the Long-Tailed Bird* by Bob Bell. Copyright 1975. Freshet Press, Rockville Center, New York.

Page 101
from "Wild Birds" by Dale C. Spartas in *The Double Gun Journal*, Winter, 1994

Page 108
from "Pheasants" by Dale C. Spartas in *Gray's Sporting Journal*, August, 1992.

Page 111
from *A Listening Walk—and Other Stories* by Gene Hill. Copyright 1985. Winchester Press, Piscataway, New Jersey.

Page 114
from *Pheasant Days* by Chris Dorsey. Copyright 1992. Voyageur Press, Stillwater, Minnesota.

The authors wish to thank Jay Johnson, Pheasants Forever
Special Projects Manager, for his thorough review of the book.

ABOUT THE AUTHORS

Steve Grooms, a field editor for Pheasants Forever, is a full-time freelance writer who has specialized in writing about upland bird hunting since 1965. His articles have appeared in *Game Journal, Gun Dog, Wing & Shot*, and *Fins & Feathers*.

Grooms, who lives in St. Paul, Minnesota, is the author of three books, including a how-to book entitled *Modern Pheasant Hunting*; *Pheasant Hunter's Harvest*, a story-telling book which focuses on why people hunt pheasant; and *The Complete Pheasant Cookbook* for Pheasants Forever.

Russ Sewell has worked for Pheasants Forever as the organization's National Director of Education since 1991. Russ began his work with Pheasants Forever in 1988 as a Regional Biologist. His primary interests are in conservation ethics, conservation education, and public-private cooperative conservation efforts. Recently, he has been involved in conducting Leopold Education Project (LEP) workshops for educators across the country. The LEP is a unique land ethics curriculum for grades 6 through 12, based on Aldo Leopold's conservation classic, *A Sand County Almanac*.

Russ completed his master's degree at South Dakota State University and bachelor's degree at the University of Minnesota-Duluth. He has a diverse employment background, which includes college program administration and four years as a forest wildlife researcher under the late Gordon Gullion.

Dave Nomsen has worked for Pheasants Forever as the Minnesota Regional Biologist since 1992. Prior to 1992, Dave worked for the National Wildlife Federation as the North Central Regional Executive located in Bismarck, North Dakota, and was a faculty member of South Dakota State University's Wildlife Department. His primary interests include fostering volunteer efforts toward cooperative habitat improvement projects and national conservation efforts. Recently, Dave has been involved in PF's legislative efforts to continue the benefits of the Conservation Reserve Program.

Dave completed his bachelor's and master's degrees in wildlife management at South Dakota State University. His interest in pheasants and pheasant management is well founded. He spent several years researching pheasants in eastern South Dakota and attributes his interest in ringnecks to his father's career as a pheasant biologist for the Iowa Conservation Commission.

America's premier gamebird. *Denver Bryan*